I Only Paint in Watercolors

For My Parents Alfred and Jacqueline

~ We have but one journey, and the landscape is forever changing. ~
~ N.

AF688568

Table of Contents

FOREWORD

As a mental health clinician, Nancy Zanicchi-Bobb trained in marriage and family therapy, cognitive behavioral therapy (CBT), Adverse Childhood Experiences (ACEs), Life Crisis Resilience Maintenance (LCRM), Myers-Briggs Type Indicator (MBTI), and Internal Family Systems (IFS). Her background in studies and training in her profession are merely adjunct to her own life experiences.

Reading her book, I find myself taking notes, noticing familiarities and similar life trials. “Perhaps the world is not so big after all,” I found myself thinking with hair-raising chills running up my arms straight to my neck. “How could anyone else understand my suffering, my pain, my despair?”

As I consumed this book, I quickly, and most naturally, grew to understand the vital lessons of how we actually choose our destiny. At times, I thought *I Only Paint in Watercolors* was written about me and how naturally the author melded her mental and emotional landscape to a fitting canvas for us all to learn from, to grow from, advance and proceed from.

As she garnered her life lessons, so did I. I gathered her “heal and repair” methods with an elated joy, knowing this author understood in full detail what it was like to fall and get right back up. Her strength and perseverance served as a personal guide, presenting me with avenues of awareness, better choices, thorough thinking, and the understanding of self-love. It is hard for most of us to acknowledge self-love; nonetheless, Nancy shows a clear path to the relationship with yourself and its necessity. Truly, one must love one’s self first before knowing how to love another.

The clinical observations noted throughout this book offer easy understanding with anecdotes and subconscious revelations. And when life becomes too much, give it up to the Universe. Such a wonderful phrase that I will never forget. Worrying about what is out of our control will only make us sick in countless ways. It is a proven fact that stress leads to illness. Let it go, so the situation can and will work itself out, naturally, subconsciously, and seemingly, miraculously.

In *I Only Paint in Watercolors*, Nancy utilizes a markedly different approach to educate her readers. Using novel concepts and novel approaches, she intergrades a comprehensive amount of information about our own pitfalls and their treatment.

K.S. Michaels ~ Author of When to Give Up on Life and Child

INTRODUCTION

The sandbox was crowded with school children. The sun was beaming down upon her while the other children scrambled about, creating masterpieces with a fury. Their imaginations quickly came to life as their little hands worked through the sand, trying to beat the bell before it reminded them to line up for the remainder of kindergarten that day. She wore a plaid dress with black and white saddle shoes, white bobby socks, and red ribbons tied to her braided pigtails. She scooped up the sand for her castle, molding and sculpting with precision. She had spent almost two recess periods working on her castle, and as she smoothed the final bits of sand into place, she stood and said proudly, "I did it! I'm done!" A little boy next to her stood up, and with one swift kick of his foot, he wiped out the entire castle.

"Why did you do that? What are you doing?" she screamed as he stomped all of the turrets to the ground. "You ruined it! My castle! My castle!"

The little boy had no remorse and walked away. As she watched him walk away, she calmed herself. Refusing to be the victim, she began to rebuild.

The next day, she went to the sandbox and saw the boy sitting there. "What are you making?" she asked him.

"A fortress for the army," he said.

She sat next to him quietly, watching his concentration and his devotion to his project. "I will help you," she said as she began to put sand in buckets and blocks. The two worked on the project for days, and soon, the fortress was immense.

On the final day, he stood up, excited and proud. "It's all done," he said. "It is all done! She stood up and smiled, and with one swift kick of her leg, she wiped it out. The boy screamed and kicked. He threw himself down in the sandbox as she stood there calmly staring at him and his now destroyed fortress.

Before walking away, she asked, "How does it feel?"

I was 5.

* * *

Throughout this book, moments of my life's transitions are captured, phases memorialized and encapsulated within these pages. These times are where I launched, leaped, dived, and experienced life itself as an independent woman who ventured into becoming a wife, mother, career seeker, daughter, and ultimately, best friend to herself. This book is about transforming mentally, emotionally, and spiritually throughout my life. When I started my journey toward self-love, I began writing daily affirmations to myself, and I continue to write these affirmations to remind myself that I still have life confronting me and I must be prepared to meet it with dignity, integrity, and grace every day. I use Post-it Notes and put them up where I know I will see them every morning. Whether one is stuck on the front door or above my coffee maker, they are there to remind me life's challenges are real and to be prepared, to be soft, to be smart, and to be humble. These self-made Post-it Note affirmations carried me through times of distress, loneliness, doubt, and grief. They also validate my strength, tenacity, perseverance, and ambition. Above all, they mirror me. They reinforce my infinite self-respect and self-love.

When I organize consulting events, I give all participants in the audience a fresh packet of blank Post-it Notes at the beginning of every lecture. When they are confronted with their own reflection every day, they begin to identify with and see the soul of their character, their patterns, and their true self with refined clarity.

This book is my collection of reflections. This is my heart and soul. Please keep in mind while reading this, however, this book is not a self-help book for crisis, anxiety, depression, and/or any psychological disorder caused by suffering. It is a book about connecting with self. It is meant to inspire and to motivate you to better connect with your soul, self-worth, value, and identity. It is about recognizing and knowing who you are by understanding how to navigate loss, set boundaries, work through transitions in your life, explore spirituality, and choosing not to suffer.

This book is about hope. This book's purpose is to share experiences with you both from a personal and clinical observation. Each chapter begins quote and a snippet of my personal journey; followed by an expression, which aims to dissect a topic; and finally, a specific focus, which can be used to practice and promote stability, safe well-being, and a soulful connection to self as you transition daily with your goals.

CHAPTER ONE: CHOOSING NOT TO SUFFER AND THE ABILITY TO REPAIR

~Loneliness is a place…
a space…
a sacred symphony for my soul. ~
N. Zanicchi

My Journey:

I was having a life crisis, and ultimately, the only person who could help me was…me. I had to be the change I needed, not just for my family but for me. This change became about my survival, and hence, my relationship with self began.

I was 27.

Expression:

I know firsthand about loneliness in a relationship, and what I came to realize is no one has to concede and consent to suffer this emotional pain. It is not a requirement in your relationships, rather it is, believe it or not, a choice. Consenting to suffering creates crisis and suffering ultimately causes symptoms of anxiety and depression. When it occurred to me, I was choosing to suffer, my whole life changed. Consenting to suffering in a relationship leads to a place of loneliness, which can be particularly difficult when you share a living space with your partner. However, something that takes true courage, strength, and self-love is recognizing that since you are already emotionally alone, you may as well live alone. This can be a hard reality, but it is a far more desirable place to be alone with self than to be in a relationship where you are suffering.

The reality is many relationships have expiration dates due to one or both partners having toxic behaviors and patterns they have not revealed or addressed during the courtship. Our minds are beautifully equipped to rationalize red flags and behaviors as our brains flood with dopamine and endorphins. Ultimately though, this emotional connection will fade if you have not acknowledged certain personality traits before committing to one another.

I have personally experienced these hard truths, and what I learned was how to change my outlook, my relationship with self, my landscape. Your landscape is built on a colorful mental palette of memories, patterns, and reflection. This is the heart and soul of what makes you *you.*

Though we cannot change another human being, how they behave, react, or engage, we can change how we respond. We are responsible for our own personal growth and change. We can share coping skills to help guide and promote change, but it is up to the other person to engage in these skills to be able to develop a cohesive and consistently healthy pattern for a quality life experience.

We must look to ourselves for answers to the choices we have made, to the situations and outcomes that have transpired.

We are our own gatekeepers, and we have a say in everything that has happened, is happening, and is going to happen in our own lives.

The truth is, in life, everyone experiences suffering, but it is our choice to stay in that suffering; without our consent, we would never truly know suffering.

Keep in mind, sacrifice and compassion are separate from suffering—do not confuse them. We sacrifice in life for our loved ones, for a husband, wife, parent, or friend. Suffering is different. Suffering is a choice. It is inflicted, and we either consent to it, or we do not. Suffering is not part of a loving, stable relationship, partnership, career, or friendship. Suffering is a disconnection from our self. Suffering is a connection to trauma we have experienced and not yet resolved.

When you choose to let go of suffering, however, you clear the path for self-growth. Through the process of loss, I let go of toxic connections, and I returned to self-care, ultimate self-love, self-trust, self-worth, and self-respect. I spent years in relationships walking on eggshells with a hard hat on, dodging emotional bullets, and enduring behaviors and heartbreak. I was choosing to suffer with my partners, but I ultimately learned not to suffer *for* them. I changed my landscape.

I began to heal and repair myself from these experiences and move forward successfully. Being alone is part of the journey to building a relationship with yourself and one that I have enjoyed. I grew to love living alone and reconnecting with myself; this deeply loyal relationship is one nobody can penetrate because it is mine 100%.

Several years ago, I walked into the unknown and created a new life for myself. I packed up all my things I had savored and cherished from all the years of my life and moved, choosing to leave behind toxic behaviors that belonged to someone else, choosing not to own or carry their baggage, choosing to be okay with letting go of love that chose suffering over me. I chose self-preservation over suffering; I chose self-love. I ended it, I made the change, I created the break, and I left.

I was alone, and it was glorious.

Focus:

(An audio tutorial for mediation is available on K.S. Michaels "Keeping a Suggestive Mind Through Meditation", narrated by Nancy Zanicchi-Bobb @ Amazon.com).

Color Breathing can be used as a relaxing resource to begin the day. Start by clearing the air in the environment you are sitting in. Light a candle or burn some sage. Find a comfortable position sitting or lying down. Turn on some meditation music, such as Peter Kater's *Angels of Hope* or songs by Diane Arkenstone, to help you relax; any meditative music you connect with is appropriate as long as you can focus and relax. Continue to take deep breaths in and out. With your eyes closed, focus your attention on your breathing. Notice the sensations as your body begins to relax. Clear your thoughts from your mind and continue to breathe in slowly through and out your mouth. Imagine the air you breathe is white light, filling your nostrils, your throat, and lungs. Then, exhale the white light. The white light spreads throughout your body, and you are now surrounded in a mist of white light. You are floating. Then, visualize a place to be (on a cloud, in space, in a meadow) and continue to breathe in and out. You are safe, you are free, and you are one with the Universe.

CHAPTER TWO:
LETTING GO, LOSS, AND DIVORCE

~We were married, and then we created a lovely divorce. Recognizing that our legal, financial, and romantic aspects were complete. We created a circle made of river rock, stepped inside, and declared our respect, our friendship, our support, our love would last forever. Until he died unexpectedly eleven years later, we kept that vow. ~

~Lori DeCiccio

My Journey:

My wedding gown was made of champagne satin and ivory lace, and seventy-five white roses fulfilled my wedding bouquet. My cathedral-length veil was sequined and breathtaking. The guest list topped 300 people, and the wedding cake consisted of two separate four-tier cakes connected by two staircases with peach and lavender roses. The fragrance of crab crepes and the vision of buttery cheeses and sauces filled the room amid flowers and candles.

The room partition suddenly opened up into a grand ballroom. The guests gasped with the magnificent visual of pink walls, flowers, and chandeliers. The orchestra was on stage playing, and the bar opened to a line of hundreds.

It was quite the party, every little girl's dream come true.

And I couldn't have been more unprepared for what I was about to step into.

I was 22.

* * *

The house was dark, the baby was asleep, and the toddler was fading, his eyes heavy as his arm swaddled a stuffed animal. It was January, and the rain had been intermittent all day.

He was gone on a skiing trip. He had called only once a few days ago. I had answered the phone with a sad tone, asking where he was and who he was with. Not hearing what I needed to hear him say to me, I become distraught, yelling and crying. The phone clicked on the other end as he hung up.

Convinced by his behaviors and my intuition, I contacted my sister-in-law, stating I thought he was having an affair. She was empathetic and listened comforting me over the phone.

It had been days now since I had heard from my husband.

I was alone.

The car sounded in the driveway, his new sports car humming into the only one-year-old home we had purchased less than a year ago.

He was back.

I heard his footsteps, his familiar walk, the distinctive step a wife familiarizes herself with. The front door opened, and he stepped in the foyer and stood there for a moment, staring at me, surely adjusting his vision in the dark.

I was on the sofa and had been crying. I could not find words without contempt, without persecution, so I said nothing.

He slowly walked in and said, "I'm leaving you," as he walked down the hall to see the children.

His luggage still in his new sports car, he left. He left me. He left the baby. He left the toddler. He left the new house. He left the commitment. He left my dream.

I was 26.

Expression:

To this day, I am traumatized by the memory of what was supposed to be my one and forever marriage and the way it ended. I immediately fell into anxiety and suffered post-traumatic stress, which I carried all through my adult years, as I learned I didn't have the coping skills required to be married at age 22, become a mother at age 23, and divorced at age 26. My dreams and family were broken. I no longer had a husband, and my children no longer had their father in our home. I realize now, this break was necessary. My first husband had narcissistic tendencies, signs I chose to ignore. Though I considered intuition to be one of my strong suits, I let my fear of the truth mask what I knew all along.

My mind was setting me up for disappointment. The ideals, dreams, fairy tales I had created in my mind ultimately never materialized. Like an oil painting on the canvas of my mind, I had painted just how it was going to be…and then it didn't happen. My dreams ended differently, abruptly. And then I learned to suffer. I chose suffering because it was far better than acceptance. Suffering let me be angry and allowed me to feel the pain, this heartbreaking ache. I held on for dear life, not wanting to remove the rose-colored glasses. I resisted change because, at the time, I felt change meant defeat. Change is hard, and it requires acceptance. It requires letting go. It takes time—years. It is a process.

When my marriage dissolved, I had to manage my emotions and learn to develop coping skills to master my thoughts, reinforce my self-worth, and ultimately empower my decisions based on my emotional well-being as opposed to settling out of fear of change. It was challenging daily, and scary being a single mother, but when you give yourself permission to love yourself, the pain of loss becomes more manageable. I learned at a very young age I would not consent to bullying (remember the sandbox at age 5), but now I had not only myself to defend and protect, but my two small children, my financial future, and what I had lost to maintain our security and stability. I was alone.

I began to focus on what I could make possible rather than what I left behind. I recognized my growth, my strength, and the new path I was forging. We are never alone when we have a strong sense of self; the relationship with self is priceless. When you embrace the change that is upon you, you become more connected with yourself. Though change is not easy, do not doubt, question, recalculate, rationalize, or bargain with your future based on what-ifs. Your past evidence is just that—evidence. What more do you need? Anything beyond is rationalization, and if you are in a bad relationship that needs to be severed, cut it off, move on, and analyze later when the dust has settled. Once enough time has passed, you will have more clarity, reflections, and aha moments.

The time to let go is scary, but it is also powerful and can bring with it insight, vision, and resilience. Your future possibilities are endless, so allow them to manifest. Allow life opportunities to bloom and transition into accepting change. Even though you may be ending a relationship, you don't have to do this alone; get the support you need to make the change. I had to learn how to be vulnerable, to ask for help. It wasn't easy, but it was necessary.

We need to understand love comes from within ourselves. To love ourselves is the first step in finding our independence, and then we can find love in others.

Our choices and how we think about ourselves and relationships are the key to changing the mental and emotional landscape. Without change, we have no progress. I had to change the landscape, so I did.

Keep in mind, there is no perfect relationship or spouse. There are, however, healthy relationships and habits you can apply to build healthy relationships, including practicing compassion, loyalty, kindness, and self-love.

If you realize these attributes are lacking in your relationship, it's time to reevaluate. Trust yourself. And if you decide to make a change, trust the process. Loss of a relationship doesn't have to feel like one. It doesn't need to be rooted in sadness. You can view it as a positive change. Moving forward, instead of painting a mental and emotional landscape in oils that are permanent, paint a mental landscape in watercolors. Paint in soft and gentle tones, ones that are adaptable and changing, just as life changes.

Focus:

Always a writer, I returned to writing daily more than ever, posting notes of affirmation around the house, in the car, and at the office. They are quick reminders that all is going to be okay, that you are going to make it through, that you can conquer the days that are overwhelming with extreme responsibility not just for yourself but for the family members you are caring for, children especially. Routine and consistent habits for emotionally healthy people are crucial for mental health, physical health, and spiritual health. Awake early every day at the same time. Stay focused, make lists, have a five-year plan for goals and finances, be solution focused, and try not to get stuck in the "problem." Be optimistic and a realist; do things that are within your reach, then adjust your goals (i.e., plan to complete that class schedule before taking an over-the-budget trip). Always practice compassion, empathy, and kindness. Always improve upon your own self-care. All these things will decrease stress and help you to achieve your goals, allowing you to be a better parent and employee. I cannot impress upon you enough how important adequate sleep is for your brain and for greater longevity. Restful sleep helps you encode all the information of the day and process it for clarity and recall tomorrow. Keep a journal and keep it private. Reflect through it monthly to see your growth and reward yourself for making it through.

CHAPTER THREE:
TRANSITIONS

~Focus on what you made possible rather than what you left behind. ~
N. Zanicchi

My Journey:
When you are going through a life crisis alone, and I was alone, you really have to dig deep and pull yourself up from your bootstraps and find your chutzpah. And that's exactly what I did. I had no choice. I was alone in a new house, miles from the city where any decent job was going to offer me any reasonable income, and I had two babies who needed daycare. My parents were far away as well, and I only had myself to pull it together. I was abandoned—we were abandoned. Thankfully, my children were too young to know the pain I was experiencing, which was somewhat of a relief for me that they did not have to experience the break between me and my husband.

Almost immediately, he was off in Hawaii with his new girlfriend, and I was home with the new house and two children wondering what was next.

I was 26.

Expression:
When you're in a distressing transitional period in your life, the first thing you need to do is decide what it is you want moving forward. Then, decide what you are willing to exchange for it, and make a plan. There is no time like the present to take control of your life and make it your own. When you are making a change in your relationships, career, or private life, make small, smart steps, not giant leaps—especially in a crisis. It is human nature to be impulsive when under a significant amount of stress, but that often has negative consequences. Think things through, weigh options, do checks and balances, speak to your therapist, consult your financier to get guidance and advice. Depending on the transition you are going through, consider joining a support group or keeping a journal. Writing goals and timelines onto Post-it Notes. Seeing those daily

visual reminders helps me to keep my goals at the forefront and reminds me to practice self-care during difficult times. Find something that best suits you and stick with it through the process.

Taking care of yourself is vital during life's transitions. Oftentimes, we fall into old habits, especially those of suffering, when transitions are upon us. I cannot emphasize enough how important it is to address suffering, especially during times of change, crisis, and challenge. While it is a natural human reaction to suppress the symptoms of suffering, such as anxiety and depression, it is best to seek help from a mental health clinician or life coach to review, talk, and confide. Do not let suffering manifest into anxiety or depression.

Everyone needs to learn coping skills throughout life, and therapy is a great place to start. Through the process of therapy, you can acquire coping mechanisms and techniques for life's challenging changes. Allow those skills to come into your life, and as you change, your suffering should decrease. We all have the ability to repair and adapt after a challenging time; we can do anything if we want to. It is important to note, however, that when things change, we must change too. You will, in time, develop the skills needed to master your direction and thus require less therapy as you build confidence in your choices and decisions. Ultimately, victory belongs to the most persevering.

Life is a series of transitional phases where we learn to adapt and adjust to whatever it is we are going through. It is common to look around and wonder how we got here, and though it is important to evaluate your choices and actions that led to certain circumstances, we should also practice embracing our times of transition. These are times of growth and change, and they give us the opportunity to practice looking for the good in times of hardship.

The most difficult part for me that intensified suffering was the loss of what could have been for all of us. My children would never know what a whole family would be. My heart was broken for them. It is in times of distress that we find it the most difficult to master our thoughts, to train our minds to think positively and forge ahead. My husband always had a way of making me feel like he deserved more, like I was in his way of some great discovery or achievement. He even went as far as to ask me one day why I could not be more like a woman friend of ours who had a successful business. I immediately felt my heart sink. Being a new mother, I was in no way motivated to become a businesswoman and climb the corporate ladder. I would often shudder in defeat, but I would reflect back on the topic he and I shared before marriage, remembering how we had agreed I would be a wife and mother and stay home to raise our children. There was never any mention of me being a career woman. I often wondered where and when that desire in his heart faded away and was forgotten.

After three months of motherhood, he insisted I return to work and place the baby in a daycare. I was young, devastated, and did not have the maturity or guidance to say what I needed to say, which was that I desired to be at home with our baby. I became resentful, tearful, and distant as I felt more and more isolated in the marriage. We definitely had an emotional disconnect as everything continued to be about him, his work, his law school endeavors, and his friends and co-workers. He had an uncanny ability to intrigue, charm, and hone a collaborative and cohesive network of people he knew he could benefit from in order to climb the corporate ladder of recognition.

I eventually sought counseling to talk about my marriage.

Focus:

Oftentimes, it is recommended that those working through transitional periods in their life seek support with a therapist or mental health professional to maintain stability and provide guidance through the transition of a devastating loss. As a mental health clinician, I am trained in marriage and family therapy, cognitive behavioral therapy (CBT), Adverse Childhood Experiences (ACEs), Life Crisis Resilience Maintenance (LCRM), Myers-Briggs Type Indicator (MBTI), and Internal Family Systems (IFS). A combination of these therapies and questionnaires may be used by any therapist in order to help counsel an individual in need, but they all may not always apply to the current needs of the individual. It can be important to understand these different practices so you can ensure a proper plan is in place to help you heal and reach your goals through therapy.

Everyone encounters adverse childhood experiences that result in emotional trauma, whether it be witnessing a traumatizing event or being part of it, such as being physically or emotionally abused, being a child of divorce, losing a family member early in life, or loss of financial income resulting in sudden life changes. Most people would benefit from knowing their ACEs score. Understanding your ACEs score can help you determine your triggers and can help you prevent further trauma by preparing you with the needed skills to handle difficult situations.

Those who have experienced ACEs may find they are often tearful; depressed; anxious; attached to things, people, and places; isolated more frequently; suffering from mood swings or bouts of anger; triggered and/or vicariously traumatized from watching the news or a violent movie; and highly reactive. You may be subject to distress and stress and have more challenging days than stable days. You may have difficulty processing information and may avoid conflict and confrontation due to the stress it causes. Regardless of how these past experiences affect you, it is important that you recognize these are symptoms of trauma and that you can learn to process your feelings and experiences with a therapist through CBT. Therapists often use CBT to decrease symptoms of anxiety and stress due to ACEs as well as behaviors that otherwise disrupt the quality of our life.

It is also key to set goals for yourself and realize stressful life experiences are traumas in the past, not the present. Do your best to keep the past in the past and look at the challenges today as new challenges, ones that can be modified and managed now. Be forgiving and kind to yourself. Recognize positive experiences you have in present time, what makes you happy, what is working, what isn’t working, and what you want to see change.

Master your thoughts, your choices, what you consent to, and whom with. We often create our mood and the situation we experience long before it happens. Therefore, being mindful of your thoughts, feelings, actions, and perhaps any consequences may help you decrease anxiety and increase positive thinking, emotional responses, and patterns.

It can also be helpful to give yourself a timeline to change and improve what you want to see changed. However, you must be reasonable with this timeline. For example, when I returned to graduate school, I was entering my midlife cycle; transitioning was inevitable and challenging. I gave myself a ten-year timeline to complete my academia, and I achieved it in five years. I felt proud of myself for not only achieving my goal but also because I accomplished it within my timeline. Make your timeline and have faith you will stick to it. Practice being steadfast in your goals, and if you find you need to adjust them, give yourself the permission to, but don't stop moving forward, even if things feel difficult.

Change takes active participation and consent. You will have to do a lot of internal work, but that doesn't mean you will have to do it alone. Work with a therapist to process your traumas and define your triggers, confide in someone you trust, and set goals and timelines that promote your growth and change. Change gets easier over time, and with the right plans and people in place, you can start to welcome these transitions with open arms.

Ruin is the road to transformation. The only thing constant in life is change. To clarify, this means we are in the middle of a life changing event, one that is traumatizing and requires us to change unexpectedly, feeling the quality of our life is being jeopardized, we feel ruined, we feel robbed, stripped of our dreams and promises made to us. Ruin is a place of no return and now we can only walk the path thrown in front of us.

There is no going back when we are ruined. This is what being abandoned feels like.

CHAPTER FOUR:
SILVER LININGS

~Never jeopardize your integrity.
Never jeopardize your credibility.
There is always more than one way
To get to where you are going…
Always. ~
~N. Zanicchi

My Journey:

Throughout high school, I dated the same boy for three years. While it was my first true, meaningful relationship, we ultimately went our separate ways before graduation. We were young, but the love was real. He will always be a part of my life because we shared so much together in our youth. I was a typical hormonal, emotional teenage girl, and he was a jock, a football player with an ego and playful personality. Our end devastated me, and I let those emotions consume me for quite some time.

Later in life, however, when I reflect on the relationship, I see it with fresh eyes. I recognize how he mistreated our relationship and used it to his advantage. He would ignore me during school hours while hanging with the other football players and cheerleaders; he played around with other girls, and then a pattern of behaviors developed. He would arrive at my house in the evening and behave like this behavior was acceptable in a relationship. Looking back, I know it wasn't, but we were young, and I think at that age we are learning to launch into trying other people on in our lives, bringing them into our home, meeting family; after all, high school is the dating highlight for most teenagers. But John Boy Walton he wasn't, I needed someone who wanted just one *girl.*

I was young and consenting to the behaviors. What kind of husband would he have made if things hadn't ended? Probably not one who would have contributed to a happy marriage if those behaviors had continued. I may have been devastated when things ended, but I see now he had actually done me a favor by breaking things off. He saved me what could have been years of pain by exchanging them for a few moments of pain.

There, I realized, was the silver lining.

Expression:

A silver lining can be found in any situation.

When the dust settles, an epiphany of silver linings will often present itself. Though sometimes uncomfortable, change and challenge thrust us into the next opportunity to grow and become closer to the core of ourselves. Keep your eye on the prize and your spirits up, and if you have to rely on others for emotional support, do it. There is time to be a hero when all is done; for now, be the warrior and get through this with your head held high.

Don't be discouraged, and do not quit. It's important to tame your thoughts, to master positivity and let go of the negativity. It's so easy to mentally direct fear and go right to a feeling of loss, isn't it? But remember, a change doesn't have to remain as a loss because a lesson can always be gained and learned from each experience. Remind yourself of this regularly as you go through change. Remain calm, practice flexibility, and stay focused. Otherwise, clarity will be delayed. Clarity is often delayed when we allow our emotions to override our logic. Emotions are powerful and while it is important to feel those emotions, we must learn to master them. We master our emotions; they don't master us.

This is especially true in times where we feel we are failing. Failing, however, is really the first attempt in learning. I often think of a baby who is determined to walk those first steps. Though the baby keeps falling down, they get back up until they've mastered the skill. They learn new techniques after each "failure." As adults, we learn our own methods for "getting back up." Every time I get beat down by a thought, a competitor, a relationship, an exam, or a memory, I grab hold of it, close my eyes, and breathe. I imagine a stop sign. I stop the thought of defeat and say, "I can do this, I am capable, and I will find a way because there is always more than one way to get to where I am going."

And you will too. Give yourself permission to pause and to feel your emotions, but don't stay in that "paused" state for too long. Keep moving forward, and if you have to look back, try to look back with a fresh set of eyes. Be grateful for broken relationships, delayed exams, tough competitors, and disappointing memories. Find the silver lining to that broken relationship and choose to let go of the emotions that kept you in a state of suffering.

Keep in mind, however, it took me years before I was able to revisit some of the memories of that particular relationship, so I am not recommending you push yourself to do things you may not emotionally be ready for. Memories can be tough when we reflect on them. Painful memories can bubble to the surface by an event in life that triggers a memory or vicariously witnessing trauma in someone else's life; either way, a memory can be as real as the present, and it can cause us to be tearful and even traumatized. How do we find a silver lining when we are triggered by a painful memory? The silver lining is that you are capable of empathy and compassion, and you are now gifted with the ability of repairing these feelings and moving forward in life.

Sharing your experience with another person you trust, for example, helps in freeing your feelings surrounding the memories. You may find this deepens your bond while also reminding yourself that you are not alone in this process.

Though transitional periods can be difficult, it doesn't mean they have to be negative. Use your insight, take off the rose-colored glasses, and look more closely. You may just find a silver lining.

When my first marriage ended abruptly, I never considered marriage would be on the table again so soon, but two years later, it was. I was happy and in love with my husband. We were still young, but he took on a woman with two toddlers, a brave commitment indeed. I felt blessed he chose me and the children after I experienced such a loss, such a severing. We had a daughter together, and we were married for seventeen years. It was a union of two people learning to live life, to manage parenting, finances, and blended families, and we definitely struggled to find our way to provide for our family of five.

My intention when writing is not to disgrace or persecute a past relationship, especially when I was also a responsible and consenting partner. Anyone in a consenting relationship has to accept accountability for their happiness as well as the lessons we learn during transitions. My goal is to share my life experiences with others so they can learn from and resonate with my hardships and triumphs. I hope that any broken relationship, whether it produced children or not, can somehow find a way to mend communication without contempt. If a relationship can end in friendship, both parties can move forward with grace.

Ending marriage or any relationship is never pleasant. Experiencing divorce at age 26 and realizing I was soon to be a single mother was traumatizing. It was sudden, emotionally painful, and there was no explanation from my spouse or, for that matter, a desire to communicate a solution—he just left. Unfortunately, the relationship did not and could not end in friendship, and I carried the weight of that pain for years. Approaching middle age, and years of humiliation at family events with severed in-laws, cold looks, and unnecessary, hurtful ignoring at functions, I decided not to consent to that pain anymore. It took me years, but I eventually stopped accepting invites and attending family events. I had this illusion for years that keeping the blended family together for events was crucial for communication, but that notion was never reciprocated.

My second marriage, however, ended mutually, amicably, and was far less painful, albeit still a loss. We are still friends and, over the years, have matured enough to know time has healed the holes we were unable to repair as a couple.

When we acknowledge friendship in a relationship and the things that brought us together as well as when we respect one another, our value within the relationship, and our individual self-worth, a separation can result in a lasting friendship. When I realized my self-worth and self-love, I began to let a lot of people go. I realized I had been consenting to their lack of respect for me, which was contributing to my lack of self-love. I have found when you love and respect yourself, your partner will also love and respect you. Love, along with trust and loyalty, is a key component of healthy, lasting relationships.

After having been married and divorced a few times, and through connecting and developing a deeper relationship with myself, I realized I needed to get comfortable with myself, alone. I learned to manage my life through my eyes, my insights, and my own life goals. I decided I would no longer consent to settling in a relationship that redirected my path for someone else's purposes. If a relationship isn't a joined union of two people looking outward in the same direction, then it isn't a relationship; it's just two people working on different goals with a different agenda. Two people who look outwardly together, share communication with emotional intelligence, trust, and loyalty, however, are Pillars, which is something I will discuss in the chapters ahead.

Discovering I would no longer consent resulted in me choosing celibacy for five years. I chose to be celibate until I met someone worthy of me, my standards, my value, and my commitment. After committing to marriage and watching my whole self-disintegrate time and time again, I knew I needed to change my landscape, the way I was functioning in relationships, and that began with changing myself. I had to learn to be my own best friend, to be alone.

This time alone was for me. Choosing to live alone was cathartic and one of the most meaningful phases of my adult life. It was inspiring, progressive, life-changing, freeing, rewarding, and transforming. Living alone allowed me to reacquaint with my true self, values, character, mental and emotional health, and what I had lost. It was a precious and unique experience. I learned to laugh at myself, laugh alone, cry when sad, cry when happy, and cry when I was grateful. The relationship I now have with myself is priceless because of that time.

I have been loved. I have loved. I have been married and divorced. I have raised children. I chose and consented to all of it. And that was all part of my journey to self. I have learned how to be kind, to be patient, to have gratitude for my home, and to love myself and others.

I used to think I had to fall in love to experience a great love, but I learned great loves can't happen until you love yourself first. When you truly love yourself and then you find someone who has done the same, you can create a foundation for a healthy relationship that can grow in extraordinary ways.

With every transitional phase of life there is a silver lining. If you look for it, it will shine brilliantly.

Focus:

Continue to journal and write Post-it Notes every day, affirming your path, your standards, your reason on this journey. Throughout my journey of self-discovery and learning to love myself before others, I created a book with the over 100 Post-it Notes. This journal not only helped me grow while compiling it, but it also reminds me of what I've worked so hard to achieve when I have moments of doubt or experience hardships. It helps me remain mindful. You too can create something similar to this to help you continue to be mindful of what you choose to consent to and to always be aware of healthy boundaries.

Keep your balance, and your inspiration can become someone else's inspiration one day. Don't quit growing.

The following are amazing go-to books to read during your alone time:

Bouncing Back: Rewiring Your Brain for Maximum Resilience and Well-Being by Linda Graham, MFT

Emotional Intelligence: Why It Can Matter More Than IQ by Daniel Goleman

Any book by Louise Hay

Are You the One for Me? Knowing Who's Right and Avoiding Who's Wrong by Barbara De Angelis

Loving Each Other: The Challenge of Human Relationships by Leo F. Buscaglia

Smart Women Finish Rich: 9 Steps to Achieving Financial Security and Funding Your Dreams by David Bach

When I first journeyed out on my own, I was midlife and had just ended yet another relationship. I sat in my brand-new space in silence, wondering what to do next. During the day, I was still interning, and I was inundated with socializing, documentation and reports, and meetings, but at home, in the evening, it was quiet, and I was alone. It was the first time that I had to create something to do for myself all by myself. My adult children grown and no relationship or companion, it was an interesting challenge. But I did it, and I wound up at a local library one Saturday afternoon, strolling down the psychology section. I picked up some books, and I came across a brand-new book in the aisle called *Bouncing Back: Rewiring Your Brain for Maximum Resilience and Well-Being* by Linda Graham; I took it home. I read it front to back, and I had what I can only call an awakening. I connected with myself. It was the one book that changed everything for me in terms of rewiring my life in the way pushed me to think beyond what I had already envisioned. I started asking myself some tough questions: What was it going to take for me to do this, what was going to be my strategy, what was required of me, what was I anticipating emotionally? I knew I had to have a strategy to make this change on a deeper level. I needed to learn to be flexible and to master self-awareness. I already knew I had empathy and compassion, but I needed to create all those other connections. What better time to do it? I was all alone. I reacquainted myself with self-directed neuroplasticity, another chapter in the book, and it was revolutionizing for me. I felt a shift happen; it wasn't immediate, but it was as if something clicked and I was able to identify options that I had in my life without the fear of the unknown.

Because I was still interning, my days were grueling schedules for three years with clients who were suffering unimaginable loss in life while I was also experiencing a major transition, I didn’t share with anyone. This book helped me see things more clearly, even during the heavy fog of my work. I was able to look at what needed to be modified and what needed to stay the same. It was an overhaul of learning how to “adult” in a different and new way, how to be resilient. I recognized that we all have this ability to repair, to be flexible, and that we truly are the gatekeepers in our lives. We are all capable of growing and making changes for the better even during our most difficult times. Reflecting on our actions, reading new perspectives, writing down things that resonate with us to revisit at other times—these are all ways we can forge the path to ultimate self-love.

I believe that we all have a predestined fate when we get here, but I also think that the journey can be adventurous, and the outcome can change for better or worse. We are the masters of that, and where our journey takes us begins with what we consent to.

CHAPTER FIVE:
BOUNDARIES

~Be courteous to all, but intimate with few, and let those few be well tried before you give them your confidence. ~
~George Washington

My Journey:

When someone has vowed to love you before God and family, words of contempt are never part of your marital vocabulary. When an agency hires you as a valued employee and holds you to a standard, they themselves do not live up to, behaviors and contempt surface, and you will realize the mistake you made not addressing the deficits before making a commitment. There are always *telltale signs; we just choose to consent and look the other way, hoping we can be the catapult for change the other person needs to be a healthy partner, friend, or business associate. We have all observed and witnessed relationships that are beyond toxic and contemptuous.*

Beware of the sociopath. The red flags and signs are indicators of manipulation and future abuse.

Expression:

The first time someone deceives you, it is a misstep. The second time and all the other times thereafter are choices. Make no mistake, they are two very distinct differences. When this happens, it is important that you set your boundaries early on. Creating boundaries in your relationships, including romantic relationships, friendships, and professional relationships, is essential for healthy interactions. Drawing boundaries allows both you and the person in the relationship to operate under known expectations, and it can certainly help you avoid heartbreak in relationships and loss of revenue in business. We all know a sociopath. It may be a friend, a coworker, or a prior romantic partner. Sociopaths are incredible navigators, lack empathy, and would do most anything to achieve their goals. They typically operate with alternative agendas and are rarely transparent. They are the great politicos of the world and usually succeed, not hesitating to step over anyone to get to where they want—in business and in relationships.

In any event, whatever it is, learn the signs and red flags and keep yourself safe.

A good example of securing your boundary is to keep your circle small and your private life private. For example, if someone at the office is pretending to be overly curious and supportive about something going on in your life, imposingly gregarious, be cautious they are not trying to undermine you professionally. This happens in family and friendship circles as well, so it is important to keep healthy boundaries. Healthy boundaries include keeping your private life private; you are not obligated to others to share any personal information about yourself, financially, private, or otherwise. Limit interactions with toxic people, including family members and friends, not just coworkers. You are not expected or required by adulthood to respond or react to questioning, and you should never feel obligated to elaborate your direction, feeling, or opinion about your private life. Remember, we allow things only if we consent to it. Anyone more interested in your private life than you care to discuss is likely gathering mental notes to use in their favor for toxic intentions. This can sabotage your relationship, relationships around you and business partnerships. Do not consent to becoming a victim of circumstance or controversy.

Boundaries are so crucial in business. If you are with an agency or large corporation, quite often management will have prospective new hires sign a disclaimer prior to finalizing employment offers. These disclaimers, usually pages and pages of rhetoric, are put in place to protect the company, their narrative, their mission statement, and the directives they have in their forever legal ease policies, and of course, most employees sign because they need to be hired and receive a paycheck. It's important for you, however, to always make a copy of everything you sign. Not all, but many agencies are corrupt with underlying agendas, so be careful. If you are savvy and play the game, take the job and continue to look for employment elsewhere.

Many times, promotions and recognitions can be thwarted due to office gossip and unnecessary meetings. Familial relationships can also be sabotaged due to unhealthy communication and a lack of respecting privacy and boundaries. Practice emotional intelligence and always be aware of who to trust to ensure you are maintaining healthy boundaries at home and work. Accomplishing this feat comes from mastering being alone and listening to your inner voice.

Take the time to understand what you are comfortable with and what you will not stand for. This will help you not only determine your boundaries but also how to maintain them.

Don't consent to allowing certain comments or actions to go unchecked. In doing so, you are making the choice not to enforce a particular value. If you are often unwilling to enforce this boundary, you need to look within and ask yourself why this behavior is acceptable. For example, ask yourself tough questions, such as, "Do I have unfulfilled expectations and old attachments? In relationships? In my career?" Begin to examine within yourself and then talk things over with a trusted person and/or your therapist. The nurturing, caring, responsible party (you) may unknowingly become an enabler by falling into the pattern of the victim caretaker/caregiver, which adds to the problem and portrays negative behaviors as acceptable or forgiven without consequence. To combat this, a boundary must be laid out.

The ability to draw boundaries often becomes clear once we've observed a certain situation or behavior, and then we can interpret it. I often ask my patients, "What did you observe in your situation early on? How did you interpret the behavior? As time goes on and there is evidence of repetitive patterns, what do you interpret now?" Set healthy boundaries for yourself so you can be part of the solution, not the problem.

It is also important to determine the type of behavior you yourself are participating in. Are you focusing on a solution when problems arise, or do you remain in a problematic space? In order for change to occur, whether in yourself or in a relationship, a person must identify the specific behavior that poses as a threat to themselves and create a boundary. Sociopaths are quite aware and precipitous with their choices and behavioral patterns. They thrive on toxic communication, and they are aware of how they behave, which is nothing short of gaslighting. This repetitive behavior dooms all their relationships, putting your energy and emotional integrity at risk. Keep a healthy boundary and be aware when you are at risk of being vulnerable.

Codependency within a relationship also occurs where dependency on drugs or alcohol supersedes ability to determine and experience a healthy relationship. If the only connection the other person has is with drugs and alcohol dependency, you are no longer a viable connection in their life. Drugs are often used as a way for individuals to disconnect from themselves and their feelings and reaching out to them can be futile if they don't want help. If you find yourself in this situation, this would be an indicator that you may need to reevaluate your role and set healthy boundaries.

It is important to continually reevaluate your position, your emotional health, and the choice and reason to remain and not leave in any relationship that seems to be problematic. Consider these questions when issues arise in relationships: Is this a phase? Can things improve, and will they? Can things change? Am I practicing rational or irrational thinking? Above all, is it safe to stay?

Sociopaths are gas lighters, crazy makers. Lacking in empathy and compassion, they cultivate and wreak havoc on people, manipulating relationships, families, and friends and playing mind games. Do not turn your back on them when you notice something is off or not feeling right.

Resentment and bitterness will enter the equation, and then anger, anxiety, and hurt will typically soon follow, initiating the need to reevaluate. This becomes a cycle, and it is entwined in toxic behavior. The relationship becomes emotionally destructive and draining, meaning it is time for a reality check. This is often the beginning of relational violence.

It is at this point I cannot impress enough the duty to leave if you are experiencing domestic relational violence. It does not get better. It gets worse. Get some help today.

Now.

Close the book, and call a therapist, a shelter, or 911. You can finish reading this later.

How can you be someone's inspiration if you are constantly giving light to someone who is intoxicated or oblivious to you and reality? You cannot. Things do not change, rather *we* must change. I don't know who said this, but I love this quote: Hope never abandons us; we abandon it. I don't like the word abandon because I know what it feels like to be abandoned, but the saying rings true. The downfall in a relationship begins with emotional abandonment, and then it becomes physical abandonment, until the union is no longer viable. When this level of abandonment happens, you feel spiritually defeated. When we give up and lose hope, we lose our ability to focus on the solution.

Solution-focused people, however, will always find a way. Problem-focused people will move away from the solution and focus only on numbing the problem. Which are you? Solution-focused or problem-focused?

There are many working components here. The dynamics for every relationship are different, but I will highlight some general solutions for relationships without addictions. If the union is struggling with miscommunication, address the source of the misunderstanding and clear the air. Focus on the *solution*. What is it you both need and want to see change? Seek therapy, create a list of reasons to be together, and remind yourself what brought you together and what you need to do to stay together. Couples therapy is a positive resource to develop a cohesive relationship with your partner.

If chemicals such as drugs or alcohol are the behaviors that need to be addressed, modification must be labeled and change through intervention is highly recommended. It would be up to the person using, however, to make that decision. Typically, an assessment or psychological evaluation is completed prior to a program, therapy, and/or medication depending on diagnosis. Again, the addict has to be the one to make the choice to get clean and sober; someone else cannot make that decision for them, so if you find you are in a relationship with an addict who is unwilling to change their habits, you must draw a boundary.

Creating healthy boundaries also means recognizing red flags in a relationship. Red flags are behaviors that indicate imminent dysfunction lies ahead. They typically show up fairly early in relationships and come in many forms. Disrespect, rudeness, name-calling, swearing, bullying, crude jokes, misdirected anger, excessive alcohol consumption, vulgar behavior in public, vulgar behavior in private, taunting, threatening, accusations, blaming, yelling, extreme highs, extreme lows, hyper-sexuality, impulsivity, pressured speech, excessive need for control, and stonewalling are all examples of red flag behaviors and can result in emotional abuse. After an emotional abuse episode, there may be a few days of quiet distance and an apology, but these behaviors often start again at the next opportunity. This is called the cycle of violence. This can happen anywhere, at home or work, and with friends and/or extended families. The cycle of relational violence is a behavioral extension of previous abuse and toxic relationships by the person who is inflicting it and who never sought help, and they are communicating their abuse onto you, whether it be physical or emotional. Did you ever have a nasty teacher in school who yelled and spit simultaneously while they were screaming at the class, or a boss who was emotionally distraught and would verbally tease and mock employees during meetings and then go in their office and breakdown and cry? Imagine how they are at home, and now, they are abusing you. (The beauty of employee assistance programs.)

In addition, red flags can be a sign of a disorder, such as bipolar or depression. Sometimes, they are a result of repressed anger or symptoms of severe abuse. Oftentimes, they are a result of alcoholism and intoxication. The abuser may have few friends and may create distance in order to more easily isolate themselves and withdraw. He/she will often attempt to isolate you as well from friends and family. They may praise these relationships in the beginning but will typically degrade and denigrate them in the end. In this cycle of violence, it is also typical for the abuser to blame their significant other for their issues or poor behaviors.

It is up to you to recognize these symptoms and signs and decide early on what you are going to do; you can either accept and consent to these behaviors and risk your emotional well-being, or you can choose to end the relationship and may even consider joining a support group to help you through this transition.

I want to note there is a difference between loving someone who has bad habits but is willing to acknowledge and change them and an abuser who doesn't believe he/she has a problem and is okay with their behaviors. These are two varying disorders. One takes a healthy approach to changing damaging behavior through resources like therapy and support groups. The other advocates for keeping the unhealthy behaviors and makes statements like, "Nothing is wrong with me, I am fine, I don't think I have a problem, I'm not going to change my behaviors, and I am okay with who I am."

If you choose to ignore the red flags, you may want to review with your therapist the reasons behind this. You may have unresolved issues of abuse and subconsciously are not aware of the need to work these out on a higher level to understand them. Red flags may not offend you; perhaps they are familiar to you, and you think you can help this person or, worse, tolerate the behavior. This, however, is a dangerous and risky position to be in.

People often reveal who they are early on in relationships. If red flags present before you enter into a commitment, you may want to reconsider your future plans. If you decide to move forward with the relationship, or the red flags become clearer later on, seek help. The earlier an individual can get assessed and receive help from a professional mental health provider, the better chance he/she has at addressing symptoms, learning coping skills, and working on having a quality life.

Red flags can also indicate present time abuse or infidelity. Couples who experience infidelity typically have many things to work through, both as a couple and individually. All too often, an affair or moment of indiscretion is blamed on external reasons, but the reality of it is this: The one who consented to the affair is the one who is responsible for it. Though working through infidelity is not ideal, it does allow the opportunity for this person to reconnect with self and really take a look at what it is they need and are missing to fulfill their life. Affairs and indiscretions are typically not intended to hurt the partner; they are actually all about the person who is having the affair and the fact that they may be emotionally depleted, lonely, and in need of being close to someone else to feel secure or to reinforce narcissistic behaviors. Unfortunately, once this is realized, the act has already been done and it is too late to take back. It is up to the person engaging in the affair to accept the need to improve the relationship with self and determine the hidden voids. It is a process, but it is one that can be successful if you are consistent, honest, and above all, value yourself and the relationships in your life.

If the relationship you have with yourself is the best relationship in your life, all the others will follow suit. These ideas also apply to the individual who was cheated on. They too must build a stronger relationship with self so they are capable of upholding boundaries and identifying when they need to be implemented. The moment you feel you have to prove your self-worth to someone, it’s time to leave or reevaluate your boundaries.

It is never recommended to remain in an unhealthy relationship, especially if you are in harm's way or in danger of being emotionally and/or physically abused. Adults, children, and extended family need to seek help and safety immediately. However, if you decide to stay in a relationship that needs work, but the work does not include physical or emotional abuse, be prepared to ride the waves, and remember, you always have options. Relationships are a choice, and you can choose at any moment to do what is best for your mental and emotional well-being. Focus on the solution, focus on you, and remember the most important relationship is with yourself first.

Ultimately, how you change your landscape may differ depending on the level of need and boundaries required for the relationship. What's most important to remember is not how you change it, but rather that you stick to your decision to change.

Focus:

Letting go of a sociopath is a power struggle, but you must do it. Once you do, you will stop questioning yourself. Your self-worth will become evident. Keep yourself safe, always have a travel bag in your car ready to go, and always know where your car keys are. Once you are out and safely away, stay away and end all contact. Change your number, email, whatever you have to do. Settle in a place where you are with friends or family and rebuild. Attend therapy, exercise, eat healthy, seek your faith wherever that may be, and meditate, connecting with yourself. A therapeutic exercise to reconnect with self during a difficult time is to write yourself a letter. This can help you clearly explain the things you enjoy about tranquility, space, self-preservation, and quiet. It can help you determine the relationship you have and trust with yourself, even perhaps, what you believe needs to improve or change. If there is too much mind chatter, begin again with some spa music and fresh air, breathing in and out, clearing your thoughts. Below is a template you can use to help guide your solution-focused discussion regarding your relationship.

A SELF-LOVE LETTER

Dear ________________________,

Today I connected with self, realizing I needed to…

____

____

____

____

____.

I miss this time, but I am so glad I am now…

____

____

____

____

____.

I want to change and/or improve upon…

____

____

____

____

____.

Moving forward, I need/want to…

____

____

____

____.

I trust that I will…

____

____

____.

Signed____

CHAPTER SIX: ALWAYS WITH YOU

~Grief never ends, but it changes. It's a passage, not a place to stay. Grief is not a sign of weakness nor a lack of faith. It is the price of love. ~

~Unknown

My Journey:

Detailed.

Alarming.

Over time, they meld into present reality. A window frame, clouds, and blue sky surrounded me as I stood in the room, a room without walls, just a window frame.

You floated in through the window frame on your motorcycle and landed next to me. I was happy to see you. You asked me if I wanted to go for a ride. I hopped on the back seat of your bike, and we flew out the window frame. We flew back into the room through the window frame and drove around the room without walls, only blue sky and clouds. You stopped the motorcycle.

Next to us on the right was a coffin.

I hopped off the bike and looked inside. It was you. I turned to you and said, "I don't like it in here. Let's leave."

I got on the bike, and we flew out the window frame.

B.S. and I were dear childhood friends. He died on his motorcycle at 15.

I was 16.

* * *

Looking downward, my sight was endless, a radial view of everything.

The lawn appeared vast and green from where I was observing up above.

Looking down,

Through eyes I had not.

I was just a presence,

Observing.

Taps was playing.

It was a clear, crystal blue sky day. Then, the gun fired—military rounds, one after the other. A white casket was placed amid the crowd of people.

I awoke, unsure of what or where I had been, where I was.

S.S. died at 17 with a military ceremony and a white casket. I was 17.

My Journey:

In March of 2016, I attended Shabbat at the only conservative synagogue on the west side of town. It was my first time there, and I wanted to see if I would like the congregation, the community. I had been to Reform services in the past at a synagogue I attended a few times during the year and enjoyed the festivities and community functions during the holidays.

The conservative synagogue was in a building that was old, in an older part of town, and only a few cars were in the parking lot when I had arrived. Eventually, eight people, including myself, were there. Most were elderly. I wasn't sure what to think of this elite group, but I sat down and listened to the elders recite in Hebrew. It was a nice Shabbat service.

Upon walking in, an elderly rabbi stood up from his chair and welcomed me as I introduced myself. He said to me, "Your parents called and said you were coming tonight, that you were new to town."

I smiled and said, "What?"

"Your parents called. They said you were coming to synagogue tonight and we should welcome you. They said they lived out of town," he said. "It was a poor connection and lots of static on the phone."

I told the rabbi my parents were deceased.

No one else showed up for service that night.

Expression:

When I think of the process of letting go after experiencing grief, I think of the words *ebb* and *flow*. The stages of grief can occur in no particular order and when we least expect them. Oftentimes, after we've experienced loss, emotions ebb and flow unexpectedly as we experience events and are triggered by environmental surroundings. Things as commonplace as music, food, fragrances, family, celebrations, church, mornings, babies, dancing, photographs, friends, hospitals, memories, traveling, flowers, smells, candles, alcohol, pets, and even the weather can trigger any of the stages of grief.

The stages of grief are as follows:

- Denial
- Anger
- Bargaining
- Depression
- Acceptance

The stages may or may not present in that particular order, and it's important to note that many people experience the stages multiple times according to triggers, emotions/mood, and how much coping skills have been acquired to recognize symptoms of grief. It is okay to grieve at your own pace; we aren't born with a rule book for loss. I make it a point to tell my clients, and myself when I've experienced loss; that we never get over loss, but rather, we move forward with it. We can seek and develop coping skills to manage the transition. Address your self-care, indulge the senses, be kind and good to yourself, and maintain a timeline to manage and complete your goals.

Remember, loss is loss. It doesn't necessarily have to take the form of a physical death; it can be a loss of employment, a relocation, a divorce, a material possession, a pet, or anything that affects the quality of your life and is a sudden change and transition.

If the loss you are experiencing now is the death of someone, I'd like to offer this bit of advice as it has helped me in my past: Write a letter to the person and from the person. The letter to the person should reflect what you need to say to them, what you want them to know, perhaps it is something you didn't get the opportunity to say while they were alive. Then, write a letter back to yourself from them. Include what you need to hear them say to you if they were still here.

When we lose love, when we experience a loss, it isn't just the person we are grieving for, it is the moments, the time, the memories, the experiences, and the words that could have been. It is this that we are grieving, what will never be again.

So, write it down. Write down what has been left unsaid and what you wish could have been said to you. We aren't always offered the opportunity for closure with loss, but we can help ourselves through this process by allowing some healing to take place through written word.

Our hearts actually ache when we are grieving. Grief literally leads to a broken heart, causes illness, pain, and emotional suffering. The heart has 40,000 neurons, basically its own nervous system. When we are grief-stricken, we literally take it to heart. It's no wonder it is so difficult to recover from trauma and loss. Our heart continues to beat and perform miraculously, however, and we eventually transition and move forward with grief as it becomes a part of our life experience. The brain encodes all the transmissions the heart signals to it, and in time, it gets better with each new loss we encounter. We learn coping skills and develop improved patterns to communicate how we feel, what we need, what has changed, and what doesn't work, and we learn to move forward with the grief, recognizing triggers that bring us to tears and then gripping our strength again and pulling ourselves up.

A lovely family lived across the street from my childhood home when I was growing up. The parents had two sons. They boys eventually grew up and left home like all children do, the wife eventually passed away, and then both sons died rather young and not too far apart. I inquired how the father was doing one day when I went to visit my mother years ago, and she said he had died suddenly and recently. I looked at her as she explained how the wife and sons had gone before him, and I said, "He died from a broken heart… His whole family was gone." My mother looked toward me and said, "You're right… He died from a broken heart." My mother always used to tell me I am a good soul. I was an empathetic child, always noticing the elder generation and feeling concerned for them if they were alone, ill, or struggling to cross a street. I remember feeling empathy for them having to live alone, having no one there to share moments with, meals with, conversations with. It was clear to me that this man died from grief, from the loss of his family.

Grief weakens the body. No matter where we are in life or what we have endured in any phase of our lives, grief is a powerful stressor that brings us to our knees, ages us, breaks down our immunity, and can bring on death. Grief is a forever life transition because it does not end; it just shadows us as we move forward with it. Learning to suffer for short periods of time and then accepting the loss are key to living with grief. The third phase of life for the elderly can be lonely and extremely long when loved ones are gone.

I feel my parents with me every day. It is something personal and private, but little things happen every day. I have read and researched many a story about contact from the other side that are miraculous and unexplainable. If it cannot be explained, it does not conclude that it isn't real. The evening at the synagogue was one of many events I have experienced in life with loved ones who have passed away. I feel blessed and protected, comforted to know I am still a part of them.

Grief and loss are part of life, inevitable transitions we must all learn to cope with. Some of us experience grief and loss early in life, others later. It is woven into the fabric of our being once we are grief-stricken. There are options for you to learn self-care and how to get through the process of loss. Love yourself and develop a close relationship with gratitude and all life's blessings. Life is a gift, so make every day count. Understanding your needs and putting yourself first is crucial when experiencing a loss. Faith and spirituality will help get you through challenging days. Sometimes, grief keeps us from being able to connect with friends, family, or our faith due to high emotions, anger, and loss of direction. Trust the process, find a support group, take the time to heal, and find your way at your own pace. Be consistent. In your own time, you will be successful in reaching a plateau that you will be able to live with. You are not alone.

Never underestimate the power of being. Energy cannot be destroyed; it can only be transferred.

Focus:

Continue to meditate daily with relaxation music. I am generally awake at 4:00 a.m. every day, and mediation in the quiet of a new sunrise has always been fitting. Whatever works for you will be fine. Breathe in and out slowly, through your nose and out your mouth.

Feel the air rushing into your lungs, the fullness of a good deep oxygenated breath. Relax. You are alive. You are well. You are on your own path, a journey designed just for you and you alone. You are doing well, and you will succeed. Do not quit or become frustrated. There is always more than one way to get to where you are going. The path less traveled may be just that path to walk. Find your solitude in solidarity and connect with self.

For anyone who experiences a void from the loss of someone or something they loved, write these letters and place them in an envelope to reflect upon later. Example letters and letter templates are provided below to help you begin the writing process.

Examples of Loss Letters to a Friend

Dear C.E.S.,

You were my childhood best friend. It was the best time in my life growing up together, sharing books and toys, swimming, doing school projects together, but mostly laughing, laughing so hard our tummies were aching. We were innocent children, loving life with no worries, no inhibitions. We had the whole future in front of us. I loved you like no other person; we were extensions of each other. And then we grew up, and life separated us. We found new friends and made new chapters, but I always kept you in my heart and never forgot you. Your obituary brought me to my knees. You died on my birthday. Was this your way of saying you will always be with me? I had a dream about you a few days ago. I walked into a room, and upon recognizing me, you put your arms around me and hugged me. "Welcome," you had said.

I will always love you.

~Nancy

Dearest Nancy,

I am with you always, and it was so good to see you in your dream. Thank you for visiting me. We will always have our childhood, and you will always be with me. We are connected forever. I love you too.

~ C.E.S.

I MISS YOU LETTER

Dear ________________________________,

I miss you so much that I…

____

____

____

____

____.

I wish that…

____

____

____

____

____.

It is my hope that …

____

____

____

____

____.

I…

____

____

____

____

____.

Signed__________________________________

I AM SORRY LETTER

Dear ____,

I am sorry for…

____

____

____

____

____

____

____

____.

I hope…

____

____

____

____

____

____

____.

I am grateful for…

____

____

____

____

____

____.

Signed____

CHAPTER SEVEN: SPIRITUAL

~You don't have a soul.
You are a soul.
You have a body. ~
~C. S. Lewis

My Journey:

The interior was reminiscent of a cabin with wood logs, furnished with splashes of green and red throughout and soft ambient light.

It did not feel familiar.

A round table and two chairs were in the room. I walked in and sat in one chair. A man in a red, long sleeve Pendleton was sitting across from me in the adjacent chair. He appeared to look like my maternal grandfather, whom I had never met. He had died at age 47 before my birth. I had only seen a photograph of him.

We looked at one another. No words were spoken. He said to me through his mind, "Don't get in the car." He showed me a picture in my mind of a purple Mustang.

I was 17

* * *

.

The Nurse's Bureau was calling frequently once I signed on for on-call CNA jobs. It was a great way to begin a career after high school, and being a young 18-year-old girl, it was a good direction to begin adulthood.

I had just graduated from high school, and summer was warming up with all of the graduation parties. Life was exciting, and the future was abundant.

The bureau contacted me, and a man was on the other end, requesting assistance at the switchboard that evening for the suicide prevention hotline and to direct calls to 911.

"I know you usually work the floor at the hospital, but we could really use the help tonight here in the office," he had said.

I accepted, recognizing it would be a good experience for me. Even though I had been invited to a party that evening, something kept telling me not to go, making my decision to accept the last-minute shift easier.

I called my friend and said I probably wouldn't be going with him and others to the party because I had decided to work.

The bureau's office was on Van Nuys Blvd, and the shift began around 11:00 p.m. The office was located on the tenth floor, and sirens could be seen and heard from the windows. The man I was working with was the same one who had called me. He was helpful, friendly, and made me feel strangely protected.

We quickly settled into a rhythm, answering emergency calls well into the early morning hours. By the end of my shift, I could barely keep my eyes open and was too tired to drive back home to the west end of the valley.

"I'm not comfortable with you driving home, but I can't leave you here in the building," he had said. "I don't live too far from the office. I can take you to my place to get some sleep, and then you can drive home when you wake up."

I hesitated but agreed it would be best. He didn't live alone, and upon arrival to his home, I instantly felt safe. I lay down on the top of the bed, and he gave me a blanket before shutting the door and heading to his living room couch.

I slept until late morning, and when I awoke, I found him sitting in a chair playing his guitar. He drove me back to my car, and I thanked him once again.

When I arrived home, I showered and went into my bedroom, feeling good about having helped with the crisis calls.

I lived with my mother who was out of the country on vacation, so I was home alone when the front door slammed shut. It was my sister, and I heard her come down the hall toward my room. When she reached the doorway, she began demanding to know where I had been all night, stating there had been an accident and she couldn't reach me. She then told me my friends had been in an automobile accident. I sprang to my feet, asking her what had happened, where they were.

She turned to me and uttered the words, "He is dead."

My best friend had been killed in his purple Mustang. My dream of my grandfather flashed into my mind, and feelings of gratitude and grief washed over me.

The man who had called to offer me work at the crisis center had saved my life. He had kept me from being in that car and had made certain I was safe from the time I arrived to the time I woke up.

It was a turning point in my life. Guardian angels do exist.

I was 18.

Expression:

Spirituality is a connection to the Universe and all that is.

I have had true, undeniable, deep connections with the Universe since childhood. These connections have helped me to never feel alone and have given me a sense of security, deep feelings of protection from something massive and infinite.

Spirituality, I believe, goes beyond religion. Religion, with all of its rules and regulations, is manmade. I believe religion is based on authority, science is based on observation and reason, and spirituality is based on both.

I truly believe spirituality is *divine* and unique to the person and holder who experiences events in their life. I have witnessed many miracles and observed many miracles throughout life in my research on spirituality.

I was born into an interfaith family: Catholic and Jewish. I was baptized Catholic at St. Joan of Arc Church in Bronx New York. Our home was always beautifully decorated at Christmas, with a glistening rotating tree, a locomotive train, and garland everywhere. I remember my mother having a menorah tucked away, and she would light a Yazarheit candle every year for her father, but that was the extent of my Judaic exposure as a child. For quite some time, my faith was a potpourri of traditions that ultimately had nothing to do with religion and were more about customs both sides of the family observed throughout the years. Today, I am just as comfortable attending church on Sunday as I am attending synagogue on Jewish holidays. I honor both sets of traditions and partake in the various religious holidays. I eventually became oriented with Judaism, embracing my mother's New York upbringing and culture. I learned that her family was of Ashkenazi decent from Russian and Polish heritage. When I had children, I decided to raise them with both cultures, leaving it up to them to decide how they chose to live their religious beliefs. Their upbringing proved to be a rich variety of tradition. To this day, I still make and prepare recipes from both cultures, from my Jewish great grandmother's secret cabbage borscht to my Italian grandmother's Bolognese lasagna during the holidays. I love them all, a mixed heritage and blessing of a blended family, rich in tradition.

In my spiritual journey, I have never wavered from Jesus and His teachings. He was Jewish, and Christianity became about His teachings and how to live a quality life based on His observations and those observations and interpretations of people who witnessed His character in those times. I received a formal education and completed a bachelor's degree at a faith-based university that introduced me to theories and critical assessments in contemporary, traditional, and literary cultures of religion. It was one of the best and most enriching experiences in my academic life.

Eventually, though, spirituality became about much more to me than religion. It was through events, miraculous events that occurred in my life, that I was led to the prospect of a higher conscious, a deeper understanding of the Universe and all that is. These moments in time, glimpses of the future, undeniable observances I came to believe are connections with energy and guidance, continued transitions and light. This desire to become more spiritual encouraged me to learn more of the history of Buddhism. I learned to meditate and reach higher levels of consciousness. When I began my meditation, I realized I had been unknowingly practicing some form of this all of my life. Meditation and words, or prayer, are our way of connecting with self-love, our soul, our essence, intuition, our energy.

I have a mantra I have incorporated into daily thinking, which is "Give it up to the Universe." When I am at a crossroad and have depleted myself of answers rather than succumb to disappointment or defeat, I give it up to the Universe. It is already written, so I release it and it unfolds where it is meant to unfold. By this, I mean, give it all away and let the Universe manage it. We have no control. I have mastered this and learned a higher power is always taking care of me. A higher power is taking care of everything.

I have found when I do this, when I let go of control, the Universe steps in and manages it. What will be, will be. The Universe is always listening, and when we pray and speak out about what we need, these words will be heard, and miraculous things will take place. We just need to be open to receiving.

Spirituality allows us to build better connections to ourselves, to the world around us, and ultimately, to others. I have found that the times I struggled the most in life were during times where this spiritual connection was lacking, during times of transition and when I needed to rebuild my relationship with self. Spirituality can look different for everyone. For some, it might look like meditation and prayer, whereas for others, it might be soaking in the smells of nature during a quiet walk outside. Spirituality has come to me in the form of dreams, in actions from others, in traditions from my family's religions, and in teachings from my academia.

It is undying energy, love, prayer, science, and faith all rolled into one. It requires us to simultaneously let go and engage, believe and question. These practices have helped me grow and, at times, have even saved my life.

If you find you are struggling with connecting to self or to others, explore your spirituality.

It does not matter what your faith is, as long you connect to the Universe by means of meditation or prayer and make it a practice as part of your relationship with self. We are all part of the Universe; we are part of the elements and stardust that formed this planet, and by God's grace, we are blessed with incredible heavenly energy, spirit, and everlasting life. Discover what it means to you and embrace new practices that allow you to embrace your spirituality.

Focus:

Meditation is a wonderful source for connecting with yourself, with your spirituality, with your faith, with the Universe, and with whatever you believe is on the other side of this life. Attempt to connect on a daily basis for at least 30 minutes. At the back of this book, I have included meditation practices for you to use. Meditation is like prayer, yet deeper. I usually have soothing music in background where I work and/or meditate, music that is soothing to the soul. Spa music or chants are also a calming source for meditation, and music can be easily filtered through Amazon. You will find a potpourri of meditation choices to relax to. In collaboration with K.S. Michaels, you can find our CD on Amazon where I have narrated a 2 CD meditation called "Keeping a Suggestive Mind Through Mediation".

CHAPTER EIGHT: PILLARS AND PLATFORMS

~ I saw Heaven standing open and there before me was a white horse, whose rider is called Faithful and True. With justice he judges and makes war. ~

~Revelation 19:11

My Journey:

In The Bible, *Revelations theorizes the Four Horsemen of the Apocalypse, figures of four horsemen, each one appearing on a different colored horse. The colors are believed to be interpreted and representative of the following:*

- *White horse: conquest, or the return of Christ*
- *Red horse: war*
- *Black horse: famine*
- *Pale horse: death*

These symbols have appeared throughout history in art and literature.

Dr. John Gottman, a well-known professor of psychology, uses the Four Horsemen Apocalypse anecdote to predict which couples will remain married or eventually succumb to divorce. The following is how he labels them:

- *The first horseman: criticism*
- *The second horseman: contempt*
- *The third horseman: defensiveness*
- *The fourth horseman: stonewalling*

The four horsemen, in both scenarios, are clearly in conjunction with one another.

- *conquest = criticism*
- *war = contempt*
- *famine = defensiveness*
- *death = stonewalling*

In The Bible, *a pillar represents the symbol and strength of a tree. Strong and upright, a pillar symbolizes strength and stability, whereas a cracked or broken pillar is interpreted as wounded, weak, unstable, or near death. As per the Hebrew and Christian religious laws, pillars of fire and smoke are interpreted as the presence of God.*

Expression:

The apocalyptic metaphor of a relationship between two people focuses on the warning signs, the holes and voids, the inability to emotionally connect.

If we replace this metaphor with the pillars that symbolize strength and stability, the focus becomes positive, symbolizing a tree of love and life intertwining one another, growing together, becoming one, in theory, diminishing the Four Horsemen altogether. There would be no conquest or criticism, no more contempt, no famine or defensiveness, no death or stonewalling because the strength and stability of the pillars will not allow that into any relationship.

As a love connection embodies two people with undeniable compatibility, so a tree stands tall and strong, deeply rooted in the ground.

When a pillar couple puts issues beside them rather than in front of them, they confront them and discuss them. They don't allow hate, mistrust, doubt, and fear to enter, and instability never comes between them. When a couple represents themselves as two pillars, they stand side by side, strong and confident; they are supportive; they have wisdom, compassion, empathy, and kindness; they're unbreakable; they do not fall or crack; and they know not of pressure.

When an individual person is a pillar of strength, they have a platform they can stand on to use as their altar to declare their principles and their position. It is not only a place for one, but two, to represent both as a couple.

Families are built by pillars. Corporations are built by pillars. Horsemen will attempt to come in and steal, rob, take, break, or kill the pillars, but they cannot penetrate no matter how ruthless, how hateful, how determined.

Pillars are built of trust and love, of loyalty, kindness, friendship, morals, and values, and pillars attract other pillars, which multiplies all of those virtues, making them extremely strong against any horsemen.

I reflect back on my previous relationships and unions that didn't survive because those virtues and values were not in place and we were not pillars of strength, and I can identify with the horsemen in those relationships.

I used to connect to the Four Horseman metaphor because they were present in all my relationships—rather, that is how I learned to connect, communicate, and maintain instability. When all you see are Four Horsemen, that's what you get.

It wasn't until I became a pillar myself and realized I am the strength and I am the stability that things changed. I am deeply rooted like a strong oak; I cannot break or fall.

No horsemen ever enter my relationships anymore because I am who I am.

Focus: Continue to remain faith-based, whatever that may be for you. Continue to connect and build your relationship with self.

CHAPTER NINE: GENERATIONAL DISCONNECT AND THE BABY BOOMER

~Watercolors can be lightened, darkened, shades and hues, mottled and muted. They are soft and flowing. They are fluid and transparent…forever changing like life. ~
~ N. Zanicchi-Bobb

My Journey:

In the corner of the garage, all neatly organized and wrapped in blankets and plastic totes, are all the "I can't let go of" things from when my three children were growing up. Time moves swiftly, and as I transitioned, they did too, growing up and becoming independent adults, now married and with children of their own. I have carted these plastic totes with me throughout my transitions in life; they hold memories of elementary school and high school years, pictures, homework, my son's clarinet, one daughter's spelling bee trophies, the other daughter's artwork and sewing projects, and all their baby clothes. Remnants of a life that is no longer. In theory, the bins are my way of holding on, not wanting to let go, yet knowing all the while these things are just material items that represent a part of my past as a mother that I am not ready to let go of. So, I packed everything in bins.

Expression:

At a time in life when I need my children the most, they are not here. The roles have reversed, and as a senior, I find my children, who are now adults, no longer need me, but I need them—a harsh reality and cruel twist of parenthood. It is yet another transition in this life that surprised me, unexpected, and like all the other transitions, no one tells you or prepares you for it. But it is here. It arrived with a thud, and now I wait. I wait for the contact, to hear a voice, to read a text, to read an email, to hear the phone ring, and dare I say, to receive a letter or a card in the post. It is a severe letting go. I no longer have to imagine how it felt for my grandparents when my parents swept us away from New York in 1962 and landed us in California. I didn't get to experience growing up with my relatives on the East Coast, though I did see them a handful of times. And now it is my turn. When we are adults in our 30s and 40s, we are embedded and centered in the thick of life. We don't realize that value of time, because time is all we have. I remember my mid-thirties were like my feet were rooted to the ground. I was in the throes of raising a family, working full-time, and trying to manage and maintain family life while being a responsible parent. I remember being overwhelmed. In our 30s, we are typically raising families, establishing values and morals, building careers, and completing goals. We don't think of valuable time spent or lost with parents or grandparents. Families get spread out, time is limited, and let's face it, being the CEO of our lives is exhausting.

Transitions are complicated in every phase of life; they bring us together, and they break us apart. It is part of life. Loss is loss. Remember, grief is personal, and letting go is a process. I will always be a mother to three wonderful human beings. Whether they make time for a phone call, text, or visit, one thing will never change: I am their mother. I remember my pregnancies like they were yesterday, the exact time they were born, and the magic of seeing their faces for the first time. I have saved every photo album, card, and video tape through each transitional phase, making DVD copies for all of them.

Life is a series of doors opening and closing from the time we are born to the time we die. We grow, change, process, observe, interpret, grow…and the pattern repeats throughout life as we transition. Letting go with grace happens as we learn coping skills. Then, grace and elegance conjoin, and we make it look easy. But it is never easy. We learn to love ourselves, and we let go of attachment and expectation. But, in truth, it is exhausting and emotionally draining.

Focus:

For parents experiencing empty-nest syndrome, never give up on reaching out to your children. As adults, they are busy raising families, building careers, and going after dreams. What we experience and long for as parents is something they won't understand until they themselves launch their own adult children into the world and feel the void of an empty room.

For seniors, the generational gap is not just a void with our children but also our grandchildren. So many parents, who are now grandparents, express difficulty communicating with their adult children due to the vast differences in how we process information, social networking, and technology. Challenging generation awareness requires patience and understanding on both sides of the age spectrum. Listening to understand is so important. What anchors these two generations now should be our familial tradition and our values, not our differences.

And for parents experiencing a void due to child separation when there is shared custody, the transition can be emotional for both parents and child. Parents have to live without their children for long periods of time, and when this happens, communication can become strained. Families of divorce know all too well the void when the children are not home; it is a major adjustment and a long transition throughout the school years. Be patient, understanding, and continue to communicate even if all attempts may seem futile. Don't ever quit.

Remember to care for yourself. There are numerous emotional support and outreach programs for parents, children, and seniors within the community, and they are extremely beneficial.

You are not alone.

CHAPTER TEN:
AS FATE WOULD HAVE IT

~Start over, my darling. Be brave enough to find the life you want and courageous enough to chase it. Then start over and love yourself the way you were always meant to. ~
~Madalyn Beck

My Journey:

The pool water was warm that summer evening in June. Music played on the radio, and I waved hello to my friends as I took off my wrap to reveal a neon orange bikini. As I stepped in, everyone in the pool looked at me through the splashes of water a beach ball made as it was tossed around.

I felt someone bump into my backside. Turning to see who it was, I recognized my friend August, called Augie by his friends, and we began laughing and hugging.

Our eyes locked, and he kissed me.

It was electric, magnetic, surprising, and melting all at once. The energy between us was undeniable. We embraced as he pressed my body close to his.

We walked to my house in the summer night and made love.

I was 18

* * *

.

In spring of 2017, I was contacted by a high school sweetheart.

We had connected through some mutual friends on Facebook. He and I last saw one another in a swimming pool after high school graduation. It was wonderful to hear from him, and we reconnected immediately, sharing topics about our childhood and our families. I had turned him down in 1978 after he had asked me to enter into a committed relationship. He joined the Air Force shortly after, and we went our separate ways for forty years.

We stayed in contact in 2017, sending brief hellos and how-are-you acknowledgements. There were 300 miles between us, and we had spoken for hours but only twice that year. In the summer of 2018, he contacted me again, and our conversations became daily. We realized it was time.

He left Los Angeles and came up to see me.

It was a warm September night. I parked the car and stood by the rear window for a moment until I could see the figure walking from the train station. It was dark, but the lamp light was just enough that I could make out his face, his walk, his familiar step I remembered from childhood. He looked over toward me, and we walked faster toward one another until we met up in the center of the street. He dropped his bag and wrapped his arms around me, and we melted into one another, kissing, hugging, crying.

We surrendered our past and let go of all doubt and suffering we had experienced. We reunited in love, with trust, loyalty, and friendship. He was home.

We married June 8th, 2019.

It's the best relationship of my life.

I was 59.

Expression:

In the five years building my relationship with self and living alone, I completed an internship, built my own home, and traveled to Europe. It was a precious time in my life. I never believed in coincidence, so when I learned the name of the street my new house was being built on was Journey Way, I knew it was all part of "my journey" and everything I have lived through led me to this point in life.

I never intended to marry again; I was content, life was uncomplicated, and time was quiet and tranquil at home.

I received a notification on Facebook from a friend wanting to contact me. I accepted the request. He and I had dated in high school, and yes, he was the love I had bumped into at the graduation swim party and walked to my house with thereafter. The boy I knew from age 12 and throughout high school, the social butterfly who knew everyone and everyone knew him. He was charismatic, animated, and loved to party, not to mention super smart in science and math. The boy who had Bee Gee platinum blonde hair and dressed like one of them would walk down the hall every day past my locker and turn his head and look at me—every day.

We reminisced about our childhood, memories with our families, friends now gone. We laughed. We cried. We spoke for hours on the phone. Our fathers had both been employed in aerospace, and he was well read in astronomy and the sciences. We shared for hours about space expeditions, planets, stars, politics, his Air Force days, his love of F-15 jets, and his career as a survival instructor. We discovered we had much in common after forty years, more than we realized.

He is kind, warm, considerate, compassionate, and does not have a mean bone in his body. He is respectful of and to all people, and he is a social and inquiring person. He mastered chivalry in the forty years we were living in different parts of the country, and in the three years we have been reunited, I have witnessed protection and grace from this man like I have never experienced. He is tough as nails yet has a heart of gold. Forty-two years ago, he asked me to be with him. We were 18, and I was not ready for such a commitment before he left for Virginia. But as fate would have it, his father predicted we would be together one day, telling him God had a plan. Though he was raised a devoted Catholic and served as an altar boy for ten years, he also knows more about Judaism than the average goyim, having grown up in a neighborhood of Jewish friends and attending more Passovers, Hanukkahs, and bar mitzvahs that I ever did.

During our courting period, which was strictly over the cell phone, I sent him information of the local veteran's district near my house, a facility that carries memorable exhibits of the war and exhibits for veterans and their families. His response to this was, "Can we get married there?"

The rest is history.

Focus:

Be good to yourself and trust your instincts. Continue to give chances where chances are deserved. Read, research, inquire, and have faith in what your heart and head tell you. Before we married, we knew we could not marry in the Catholic Church since we had both been previously married. Our dear friend, who is also the lead chaplain at the V.A. hospital near our home, agreed to marry us. We participated in a series of tests, much like the MBTI tool used as a guide to understanding personality types. The results of the exam were calculated, and the chaplain informed us he had never seen a more compatible couple as we scored so closely together.

We knew we had the energy, compatibility, and dynamic intuition between us after all these years. We knew it because we knew ourselves.

Below are worksheets aimed at helping you discover ways to better your relationship with self. Take your time and fill each one out honestly and thoroughly.

Worksheet Template 1: Goals for Relationship with Self

On this worksheet, write down what it is you desire and what you want to experience. Spend as much time as possible with this. You will use this as a guide for your future goals. It's all about connecting with self, so write down everything that you can think of that you want to experience. For example, when I did this, I wrote down that it is crucial to live alone for at least two years to develop and connect with self. I wrote I wanted to travel. I wrote that, when it is time, I will only consent to someone with standards similar to my own. I wrote that I wanted to build a house on my own, I wanted to invest, I wanted to complete a class in finance, etc.

Worksheet Template 2: What to Avoid

Avoid things like illness, danger, pain, conflict, complicated relationships, etc. Always embrace your thoughts as awareness. This is your intuition. Pay attention to it; it is your friend and guide. If something doesn't fit or feel right, you are usually right. Pick up the beat and regroup.

Worksheet Template 3: Consent

What I will consent to:

Example: I consent to safe, healthy relationships after I have given them ample time to reveal any unhealthy patterns that may otherwise conflict with my healthy boundaries.

What I do not consent to:

Example: I do not consent to complicated relationships, intrusive unhealthy boundaries, toxic relationships…

Life Goals Work Sheet

On this page write down what you want out of *your* life…your long-term goals.

What I want from *my* life:

____

____

____

____

____

____

____

I want to live to age: ________

CONCLUSION

We don't arrive in the world with instructions for life. We are born and then dive into transition after transition. Time moves quickly, and we often cannot stop to deal with every loss or event as they happen. Eventually, over time and as events are repressed, they surface through emotions, anxiety, and depression; they can be triggered by something as familiar as a moment present in time. And we begin to process. These changes can come as painful realizations, but they can also be healing. As we remember, regret, laugh, and cry, we experience life. And life truly is like watercolors—forever fluid, evolving.

It is my hope that this book helps you through these watercolors of life and that you can find resolve while connecting to my life story. May you find answers to unresolved sadness, loneliness, and loss. This book is my pain, my joy, and my soul. I hope it brings you comfort when grieving, epiphanies, and centeredness as you connect with self through the words on the pages. Ultimately, I hope this book helps you build the best relationship with yourself. If you live a life that is rich with truth and loyalty to self, you will never be alone.

You will always have you.

~To exist is to change, to change is to mature, to mature is to go on creating oneself endlessly. ~

~Henri Bergson

Additional Resources

The following resources derived from Power Points I created provide additional insight and motivation in a concise and abbreviated manner. The three presentations are titled Consenting, I Do Not Consent, and Change the Landscape. In the Consenting PowerPoint, you will find information on how to connect with self and draw healthy boundaries. In the I Do Not Consent PowerPoint, you will be given insight into common red flags, the health issues that arise from stress, and the value of self-love. Finally, in the Change the Landscape PowerPoint, you will gain knowledge about mindfulness and the practice of self-affirmations. Each of these PowerPoint presentations can be used as resources and reminders, and it is my hope they will provide you with both knowledge and encouragement.

DAILY BASIC NEEDS

- Oxygen
- Water
- Food
- Shelter
- Security/Safety
- Love

HEALTHY BOUNDARIES

- Respect
- Compassion
- Empathy
- Kindness
- Positivity
- Goals
- Learning
- Advanced Listening Skills
- Coping Skills
- Keep Private Life Private
- Keep Your Circle Small
- Master Your Thoughts
- Moral Compass Daily

INTUITION

- Mindfulness
- Intuition is Awareness
- Beware of Red Flags
- Embrace the Moment
- Trust the Process of Every First Impression (Signs)
- Does your Heart & Gut Fit your Thoughts
- Beware of the Wolf in Sheep's Clothing
- Healthy Patterns Create Cognitive Connection
- Goodness in, Goodness out (vs. Garbage in, Garbage Out)
- Create Healthy Networks (Lecture, Forums, Consulting)
- Avoid Hyperbole
- Moral Compass Daily

DAILY SELF-CARE

- MEDITATE 30 MINUTES IN THE A.M.
- MEDITATE 30 MINUTES IN THE P.M.
- HYDRATE DAILY
- LISTEN TO MUSIC THAT SOOTHES & RELAXES YOU
- EAT SMART, BALANCED & NUTRITIONAL
- PEACEFUL, TRANQUIL BATH/SHOWER WITH SALTS
- RESTFUL EVENING SLEEP WITH COOL AIR

EMBRACE TRANSITION

- TRANSITION IS DAILY
- EMBRACE CHANGE
- BE GENTLE WITH YOURSELF
- ALLOW YOURSELF TO BE VULNERBLE TO EMOTION
- CRY, LAUGH, REFLECT, RESONATE
- LISTEN TO UNDERSTAND
- TAKE MENTAL NOTES
- WRITE POST-IT-NOTES, JOURNAL
- YOUR BRAIN IS A POWER TOOL, USE IT TO CREATE POSITIVE CHANGE

CAPTURE THE DAY

- AFFIRMATIONS
- READ, JOURNAL, WRITE, POST-IT
- BE CREATIVE WITH WHAT YOU LOVE DOING
- PAINT, COOK, GARDEN, BAKE, PHOTOGRAPH
- STAY ORGANIZED
- MORAL COMPASS

The day is encoded in your brain, allow yourself the sleep required to process this information for neuroplasticity, you are creating positive neurological patterns for an improved life

Note: Every template I have MORAL COMPASS at the end of every resource. Our MORAL COMPASS is our navigator, our guiding light, our window to the world. The needle is pointing the direction to every situation in our life, daily. Pay attention to it and understand the role of YOUR CONSENT in everything that happens to you.

I DO NOT CONSENT…AND OTHER ATROCITIES

- DISRESPECT
- BULLYING
- INTIMIDATION
- COERCING
- MANIPULATION
- GROUP THINK VS. INDIVIDUAL THINK
- COMPLICATED RELATIONSHIP (friends, family, office)
- OBVIOUS MISREPRESENTATION
- CORRUPTION
- DANGER
- ILLEGAL BEHAVIOR / SEXUALIZED BEHAVIOR

STRESS CREATES

- ILLNESS
- SELF-DOUBT
- CONFUSION
- MISINTERPRETATION
- EMOTIONAL OUTBURSTS
- INSOMNIA
- IMPATIENCE
- MISCOMMUNICATION
- CLOUDED JUDGMENT
- UNUSUAL BEHAVIORS
- PRESSURED SPEECH
- OVERSIGHTS / OVER THINKING
- EMOTIONAL EATING, DRINKING, SMOKING

WHEN NOT TO CONSENT

When we are in a position of pre-consent or considering a direction to something that is negative, stress moves in, and we may feel something is off, something doesn't feel right, much like an anxiety attack. Be mindfully aware to your body, it is talking to you. The better connection you have with self, the easier this is to recognize. Adjust your MORAL COMPASS and pay attention to your social environment.

- Heart rate increases
- Sweating
- Feeling Anxious, confused
- Dry Mouth
- Increased Breathing

VALUES…OUR CONNECTION TO SELF THE GOLDEN THREAD

Every time we consent to something harmful and toxic, the golden thread of life is at stake. It weaves into the fabric of our daily life until we stop allowing ourselves to experience others abuse. All the values held near and dear with connection to self, begin to diminish and are jeopardized. Values are:

- SELF WORTH
- GOOD HEALTH
- FRIENDS & FAMILY
- EMPLOYMENT / FINANCES
- SAFETY / SECURITY
- CONNECTION TO SELF / INTEGRITY

When Jeopardized They Will be replaced with:

- INSTABILITY / INSECURITY
- TOXIC COMMUNICATION / SELF-DOUBT
- DECREASE IN SAFETY
- LOSS OF FINANCES
- LOSS OF CONNECTION WITH SELF
- INCREASED ANXIETY
- INCREASED STRESS
- INFILTRATION OF ILLNESS OR WORSE

What Needs to Change?

- Relationships?
- Feelings of Diminished Self-Worth?
- Disillusionment?
- Career?
- Improved Health?
- Bad Habits & Patterns?
- Self-Confidence?

What are you Willing to Give Up?

- Intimacy?
- Large Groups?
- Bad Habits?
- Destructive Patterns?

What is Working?

- Small Circle of Friends?
- Privacy?
- Finding Your Space?
- Meditation & Connection to Self?
- Education?
- Supportive Research?

SELF-LOVE

- I AM #1
- I AM WORTHY
- I AM SMART
- I AM CONFIDENT
- I AM SO COMPETENT
- I CAN DO THIS
- I WILL ALLOW MYSELF TO BE VULNERABLE

ALONE TIME

- TIME ALONE IS PRECIOUS
- TIME ALONE ALLOWS FOCUS & TRANQUILITY
- TIME ALONE IS SELF SUPPORTIVE & SELF-SUFFICIENT
- TIME ALONE IS HEALTHY, I AM STRONG
- TIME ALONE IS MY HEALTHY BOUNDARY
- TIME ALONE IS SPIRITUAL, I AM NOT ALONE

POSITIVITY

- I PRACTICE POSITIVE SELF-CARE
- I TREAT SELF WITH LOVE & PAMPERING
- ALWAYS BE KIND; IT COMES BACK TO YOU
- BE PATIENT
- BE GENTLE
- STAY ORGANIZED (ALWAYS)
- KEEP ROUTINE (ALWAYS)
- ALWAYS BE LED BY YOUR MORAL COMPASS

PATIENCE

Patience truly is a virtue. Don't leap where you can walk. In other words, take your time and savor this time alone. Literally smell the roses, plant a garden, paint a garden using watercolors and change the landscape. Remember, the grass isn't greener on the other side. Stay in your Castle and climb the Ivy you are building. Be rational and reasonable. Make a timeline and try to stay on it. You can make changes as you wish, however, if you are more adaptable to another plan for yourself, it is OK to change your mind. That isn't self-doubt; it's being self-aware and using your intuition. Never jeopardize your next step.

Nancy Zanicchi-Bobb

CHANGE THE LANDSCAPE
…IT IS FOREVER CHANGING

Without change we have no progress, paint a mental and emotional landscape, use watercolors of soft and gentle tones, be adaptable and flexible to change.

ADJUST AS LIFE CHANGES

About the Author

Nancy is a respected advisor in counseling psychology, an advocate, and an instructor. She works with married and unmarried couples, as well as with individuals and families, to develop improved coping skills through and for life's transitions. She earned a master's degree in counseling psychology, specializing in marriage and family therapy, and a bachelor's in leadership. A graduate from the University of La Verne School of Law Paralegal Studies Program, she has also worked with couples in family law and has assisted couples with mediation and child custody plans.

She reaches out to all age spectrums, lecturing and speaking on life transitions and the process of self-love and letting go. She is an advocate for the elderly community, for which she refers to as the forgotten generation, and continues to reach out to seniors and communities for those in need of counseling who are experiencing and living with generational transition.

Offering support during life transitions for men, women, and children who have championed through adverse childhood experiences, trauma, loss, and challenging times, Nancy emphasizes the importance of constant self-awareness and how our relationship with self is always number one and the beginning of everything we encounter and embrace as we transition in life.

Nancy has three adult children and presently five grandchildren. While a native of Bronx, New York, she has resided and worked in California most of her life. She lives with her husband in California.

This book will soon be available in audio and is the first in a series of three volumes.

WHEN DO I NEED SUPPORT OUTSIDE MYSELF?

- *DEPRESSION MORE THAN 2 WEEKS*
- *INCREASED ANXIETY*
- *INSOMNIA*
- *DECREASED APPETITE/WEIGHT LOSS*
- *INCREASED SADNESS / TEARFULNESS*
- *ILLICIT DRUG USE, ALCOHOL CONSUMPTION*

PLEASE CONTACT MENTAL HEALTH PROFESSIONAL, SUPPORT GROUP AND/OR CRISIS INTERVENTION IN YOUR COMMUNITY FOR IMMEDIATE CONSULTATION AND ASSESSMENT.

Starry Night Publishing

Everyone has a story...

Don't spend your life trying to get published! Don't tolerate rejection! Don't do all the work and allow the publishing companies reap the rewards!

Millions of independent authors like you, are making money, publishing their stories now. Our technological know-how will take the headaches out of getting published. Let Starry Night Publishing take care of the hard parts, so you can focus on writing. You simply send us your Word Document and we do the rest. It really is that simple!

The big companies want to publish only "celebrity authors," not the average book-writer. It's almost impossible for first-time authors to get published today. This has led many authors to go the self-publishing route. Until recently, this was considered "vanity-publishing." You spent large sums of your money, to get twenty copies of your book, to give to relatives at Christmas, just so you could see your name on the cover. Now, however, the self-publishing industry allows authors to get published in a timely fashion, retain the rights to your work, keeping up to ninety-percent of your royalties, instead of the traditional five-percent.

We've opened up the gates, allowing you inside the world of publishing. While others charge you as much as fifteen-thousand dollars for a publishing package, we charge less than five-hundred dollars to cover copyright, ISBN, and distribution costs. Do you really want to spend all your time formatting, converting, designing a cover, and then promoting your book, because no one else will?

Our editors are professionals, able to create a top-notch book that you will be proud of. Becoming a published author is supposed to be fun, not a hassle.

At Starry Night Publishing, you submit your work, we create a professional-looking cover, a table of contents, compile your text and images into the appropriate format, convert your files for eReaders, take care of copyright information, assign an ISBN, allow you to keep one-hundred-percent of your rights, distribute your story worldwide on Amazon, Barnes & Noble and many other retailers, and write you a check for your royalties. There are no other hidden fees involved! You don't pay extra for a cover, or to keep your book in print. We promise! Everything is included! You even get a free copy of your book and unlimited half-price copies.

In nine short years, we've published more than four thousand books, compared to the major publishing houses which only add an average of six new titles per year. We will publish your fiction, or non-fiction books about anything, and look forward to reading your stories and sharing them with the world.

We sincerely hope that you will join the growing Starry Night Publishing family, become a published author, and gain the worldwide exposure that you deserve. You deserve to succeed. Success comes to those who make opportunities happen, not those who wait for opportunities to happen. You just have to try. Thanks for joining us on our journey.

www.starrynightpublishing.com

www.facebook.com/starrynightpublishing/

www.ingramcontent.com/pod-product-compliance
Lightning Source LLC
LaVergne TN
LVHW022311200926
848481LV00004B/1281